Nonfiction Reading and Writing Workshops

Compare-Contrast Article

Teacher's Guide

Comprehension Strategy
Asking Questions

Writing Focus
Compare-Contrast Essay

Program Consultants

Stephanie Harvey
P. David Pearson

Picture Credits

Page 4 (left) courtesy Stephanie Harvey, courtesy, P. David Pearson; page 7 © Breck P. Kent, (inset) David M. Schlessor/Photo Researchers, Inc.; page 9 (first row) Kevin Schafer/Getty Images, Michael Nichols/National Geographic Image Collection, (second row) © Gerry Ellis/Minden Pictures, Scotts Bluff National Monument, (third row) ANT Photo Library, Andrew Chapman Photography bigcheez@vicnet.net.au; page 11 (top left) Culver Pictures, NY; page 11 (bottom right) M. & C. Denis-Huot Bios/Auscape; pages 15, 39 Christopher Arnesen/Getty Images; page 29 photolibrary.com; page 30 Getty Images; page 32 Dennis Cox/ChinaStock; page 33 Jodi Cobb/ National Geographic Society Image Collection; page 34 Yann Layma/Getty Images; page 35 Oriental Museum, Durham University/Bridgeman Art Library; page 36 Christie's Images/Bridgeman Art Library; page 37 Phil Schermeister/National Geographic Society Image Collection

Info Pal icon art by John Haslam.

Produced through the worldwide resources of the National Geographic Society, John M. Fahey, Jr., President and Chief Executive Officer; Gilbert M. Grosvenor, Chairman of the Board; Nina D. Hoffman, Executive Vice President and President, Books and Education Publishing Group.

Prepared by National Geographic School Publishing

Ericka Markman, Senior Vice President and President, Children's Books and Education Publishing Group; Steve Mico, Vice President, Editorial Director; Marianne Hiland, Executive Editor; Jim Hiscott, Design Manager; Kristin Hanneman, Illustrations Manager; Matt Wascavage, Manager of Publishing Services; Sean Philpotts, Production Manager.

Manufacturing and Quality Control

Christopher A. Liedel, Chief Financial Officer; Phillip L. Schlosser, Director; Clifton M. Brown III, Manager.

Program Consultants

Stephanie Harvey, National Educational Consultant, Colorado; P. David Pearson, Professor and Dean, University of California, Berkeley.

English Language Learners Consultant

Josefina Tinajero, Assistant Dean, College of Education, University of Texas at El Paso

Program Development

Mary Anne Wengel

Book Development

Morrison BookWorks

Book Design

Steven Curtis Design

Published by the National Geographic Society
1145 17th Street, N.W.
Washington, D.C. 20036-4688

ISBN: 0-7922-4519-9

Second Printing June 2004
Printed in Canada.

Contents

About the Program

Part 1

Reading Workshop
Asking Questions

Part 2

Writing Workshop
Compare-Contrast Essay

Extend

About the Program

Goals

Teachers everywhere agree: students need more support and practice in reading and writing nonfiction. The *Nonfiction Reading and Writing Workshops* make up a program designed to provide explicit instruction in the strategies students need to read and write different kinds of informational text. The program develops the skills and strategies students need to

- Use comprehension strategies proven effective, based on research studies
- Understand a variety of nonfiction forms and genres

- Use the text features found in nonfiction
- Use the writing process for nonfiction forms
- Connect reading and writing

Program Consultants

The *Nonfiction Reading and Writing Workshops* make up a research-based program that incorporates the best teaching and learning practices that have been proved effective through carefully designed educational research. The program has been developed in conjunction with Stephanie Harvey and P. David Pearson, two nationally recognized educators and researchers.

Stephanie Harvey

Stephanie Harvey is a consultant and staff developer for the Public Education and Business Coalition in Denver, Colorado. She works with educators around the country, leading workshops and conducting classroom demonstrations. *Nonfiction Matters* and *Strategies That Work: Teaching Comprehension to Enhance Understanding* are two of her recent books.

P. David Pearson, Ph.D.

P. David Pearson, Ph.D., is the Dean of the Graduate School of Education at the University of California, Berkeley. He is a former co-director of the Center for the Study of Reading and president of the National Reading Conference and the National Conference of Research in English. His numerous publications include the *Handbook of Reading Research,* now in its third edition, and *Reading Difficulties: Instruction and Assessment.*

Research-Based Instruction

The findings from numerous research studies and from the National Reading Panel's comprehensive review of educational research conclude that

Comprehension can be improved by explicit instruction that helps readers use specific comprehension strategies.

The *Nonfiction Reading and Writing Workshops* provide this instruction. This research-based program incorporates the best practices that have been proven effective in nonfiction literacy instruction.

Good readers are active and purposeful readers who use a range of comprehension strategies to make sense of text. These strategies can be taught through carefully designed instruction. Each Workshop in the *Nonfiction Reading and Writing Workshops* begins with an explicit explanation of a comprehension strategy that is modeled by the teacher and followed by opportunities for students to use the strategy in guided and independent practice. The program develops these six reading comprehension strategies.

Reading Comprehension Strategies

Making Connections taps into students' prior knowledge and helps them connect what they read to personal experiences, other texts they have read, and general world knowledge.

Asking Questions encourages students to generate their own questions as they read, look for answers that may or may not be in the text, and self-monitor their own comprehension.

Visualizing shows students how to create mental images of what they are reading.

Making Inferences guides students in filling in the missing information that the writer has not stated in the text. This strategy helps students move beyond literal comprehension.

Determining Importance helps students recognize the big ideas and critically evaluate the author's intent. Students develop the ability to sift interesting details from stated and unstated main ideas in text.

Synthesizing helps students summarize the important ideas so they can think about what the information means to them and develop opinions, perspectives, and new ideas.

Components

Student Books

- The fifteen *Nonfiction Reading and Writing Workshops* are organized into three levels, according to the difficulty of the reading selection and application of the strategy.

- Each Workshop focuses on a specific reading comprehension strategy, as well as characteristics of one kind of nonfiction writing.

Level A	Level B	Level C

Level A

Personal Narrative
- Comprehension Strategy
Visualizing
- Writing Focus
Personal Narrative

Compare-Contrast Article
- Comprehension Strategy
Asking Questions
- Writing Focus
Compare-Contrast Essay

Articles Using Sequence
- Comprehension Strategy
Determining Importance
- Writing Focus
How-to Report

Interview
- Comprehension Strategy
Making Inferences
- Writing Focus
Interview

Visual Information
- Comprehension Strategy
Making Connections
- Creating Visuals
Maps

Level B

Cause-Effect Article
- Comprehension Strategy
Asking Questions
- Writing Focus
Explanation

Description
- Comprehension Strategy
Visualizing
- Writing Focus
Description

Informational Article
- Comprehension Strategy
Determining Importance
- Writing Focus
Informational Article

Feature Story
- Comprehension Strategy
Making Connections
- Writing Focus
Feature Story

Visual Information
- Comprehension Strategy
Making Inferences
- Creating Visuals
Diagrams

Level C

Problem-Solution Article
- Comprehension Strategy
Synthesizing
- Writing Focus
Problem-Solution Essay

Letters and Journals
- Comprehension Strategy
Making Inferences
- Writing Focus
Letters and Journals

Biographical Sketch
- Comprehension Strategy
Asking Questions
- Writing Focus
Biographical Sketch

Informational Article
- Comprehension Strategy
Making Connections
- Writing Focus
Informational Article

Visual Information
- Comprehension Strategy
Determining Importance
- Creating Visuals
Graphs

Teacher's Guides

- Each Workshop has a separate Teacher's Guide.

- Teacher's Guides provide explicit instruction and sample modeling for reading comprehension and writing strategies.

- Additionally, Teacher's Guides provide mini-lessons, strategies and materials for meeting individual needs, graphic organizers, and more.

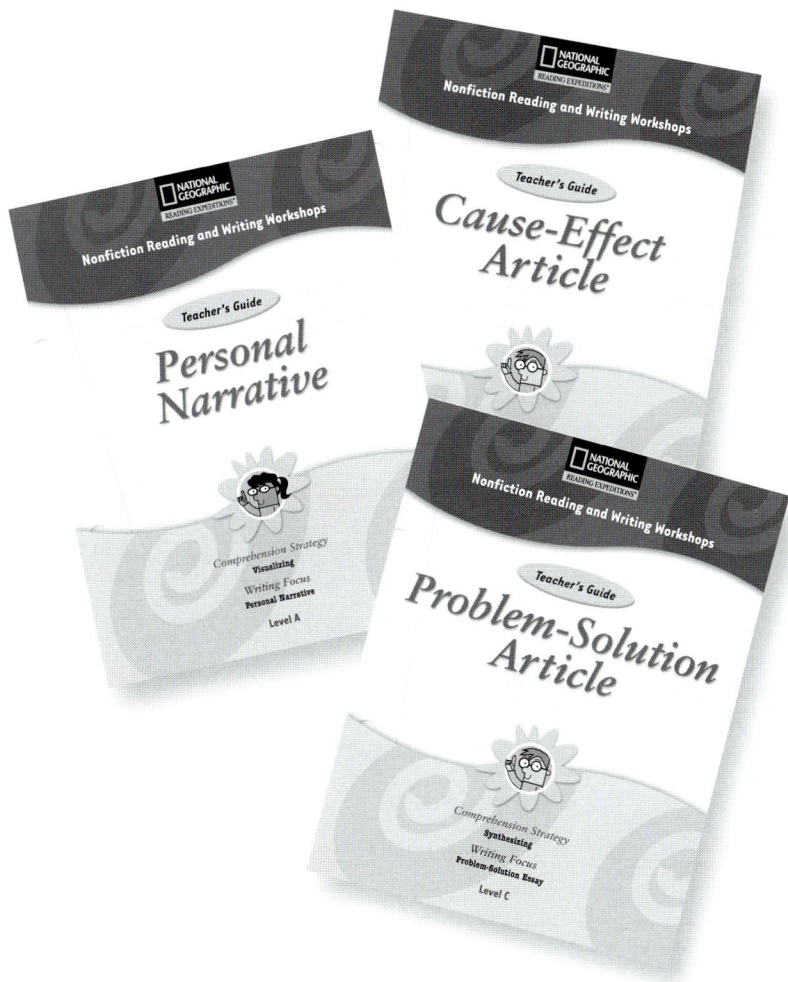

Reading Comprehension and Writing Transparencies

- A set of transparencies is available for modeling reading comprehension and writing strategies.

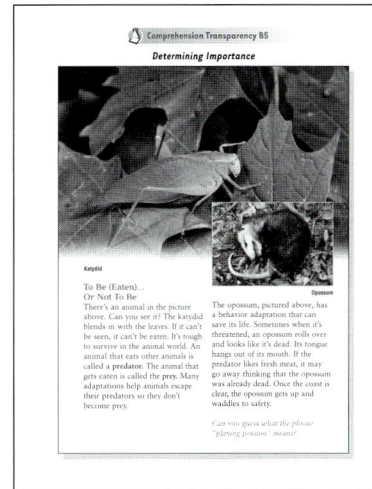

Managing Instruction

Flexibility

The *Nonfiction Reading and Writing Workshops* can easily become part of your regular reading and writing routines. You can use the Workshops in several ways.

- **Full Unit of Instruction** Use one of the Workshops as a 2–3 week reading and language arts unit of instruction. With this model, students might spend 4–5 days in the Reading Workshop before moving on to the Writing Workshop. Students can wrap up the unit by selecting from the "On Assignment" activities.

- **Reading Genre Study** Teach the Reading Workshop as a nonfiction genre study.

- **Writing Genre Study** Teach the Writing Workshop to focus on writing a specific nonfiction writing form. Help students prepare for formal writing tests.

- **Extend the Reading Workshops** Use the Reading Workshops to support students as they learn specific comprehension strategies. Provide additional strategy practice by using recommended titles from *Reading Expeditions*.

- **Supplement Core Instruction** Use the Workshops to supplement reading and writing skills and strategies introduced in core programs. The Workshops can be used in any order and can be easily integrated into your instructional sequence.

- **Center Work** Put copies of the Workshops in the Reading Center for students who need independent activities related to your reading and writing instruction.

Grouping Options

All students will benefit from your modeling of strategic reading, note-taking, responding, and following the steps of the writing process. Students learn best when they see what other readers and writers do. So, even if you plan to use the Workshops for independent work, set aside some time to model the strategies for students. Here is an instructional routine you might consider.

Introduce the Workshop to the Whole Group
- Teach the genre
- Model the reading strategy
- Model taking notes

Work with Individuals or Small Groups
- Guide practice
- Provide independent practice
- Use the mini-lessons for targeted instruction
- Use the easier selection for strategy practice

Bring the Whole Group Back Together
- Model using the graphic organizer to check understanding
- Pair students for sharing oral responses
- Model writing a response to the reading

Meeting Individual Needs

Nonfiction Reading and Writing Workshops are designed to support a wide range of students. You support students when you show them how to accomplish tasks, rather than just tell them. The *Nonfiction Reading and Writing Workshops* help you reach all students. The Teacher's Guides provide:

- Models for using reading and writing strategies

- Mini-lessons for extra support in reading comprehension strategies, using text features, and topics in writing

- An additional easier reading selection you can use with students who need more support

More Reading

The *Nonfiction Reading and Writing Workshops* include authentic reading selections from *Reading Expeditions, Windows on Literacy,* and *National Geographic Explorer!* magazine. These can be ordered from National Geographic and can be used to support your teaching in reading and writing nonfiction. For more information, call 1-800-368-2728.

Assessment

The Reading and Writing Workshops help you to informally assess student progress.

- **Check Understanding** offers an opportunity to check whether students have comprehended the important ideas and content presented in the reading selection. Sample answers shown on graphic organizers are provided on page 17 of the Teacher's Guide.

- **Write a Response** Use the criteria presented on page 18 of the Teacher's Guide to evaluate students' written responses to the reading selection.

- **Assess Writing** Use the rubric presented on page 24 of the Teacher's Guide to evaluate the writing products done in the Writing Workshops. The rubric uses six writing traits as a basis for evaluation.

◆ ELL Supporting English Language Learners

To be successful in mainstream academics, students acquiring English need to understand grade-level content as well as acquire the academic language to access that content. *Nonfiction Reading and Writing Workshops* help all students develop the skills and strategies they need to access and comprehend content-area reading. The program supports English Language Learners by

- Developing learning strategies that empower students to become more independent and self-directed in their learning

- Focusing on nonfiction text structures and features so that students see how to access the content in informational writing

- Using pictures and other visuals to provide comprehensible input

- Using graphic organizers as tools for understanding content and the connections among ideas

- Providing explicit instruction, modeling, and practice of key comprehension strategies

- Offering less challenging reading selections for initial strategy instruction

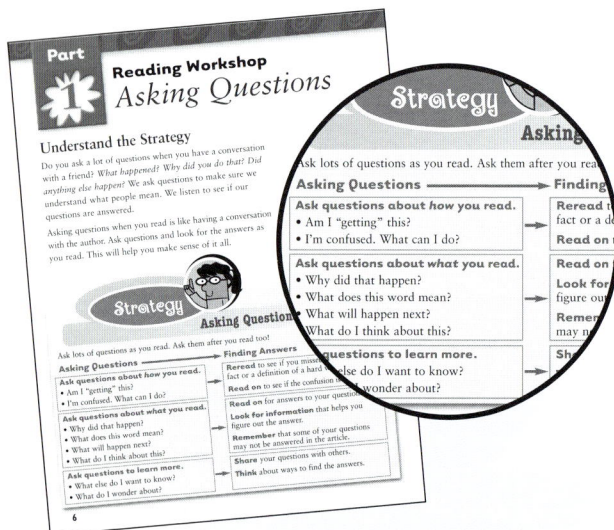

ELL Each Workshop provides explicit instruction and practice in a reading comprehension strategy. Students develop independent learning strategies.

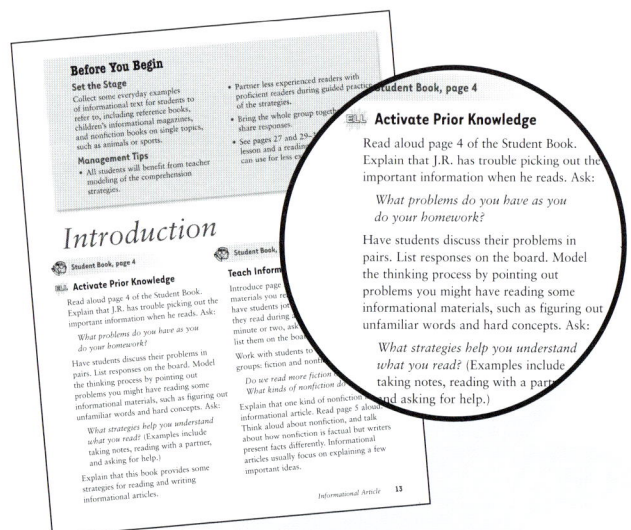

ELL Building background at the start of each lesson taps into students' backgrounds and connects what they already know to what they are learning.

ELL Annotations support students in acquiring vocabulary and understanding how text features, such as titles and photographs, clarify content.

ELL Graphic organizers help students organize ideas and see ways concepts are related.

ELL Mini-lessons in the Teacher's Guide offer explicit instruction in a range of strategies that support English Language Learners.

ELL Using an easier reading selection for initial reading strategy instruction allows students to develop grade-level skills.

Overview

Objectives

Reading Strategies

- Learn the strategy of **asking questions**
- Use **text features** to predict content: subheads, words in bold print, photographs, captions
- Use a **graphic organizer** to take notes
- Identify characteristics of **compare-contrast articles**

Writing Strategies

- Use the **writing process** to write a compare-contrast essay

- Use **prewriting** strategies: lists, Venn diagram, ways of organizing information
- Use **revising** strategies
- Use **traits** to evaluate writing
- Write in **response** to reading

Meeting Individual Needs

Reading and Writing Mini-Lessons
- Use Text Features to Predict Content
- Read in Sections
- Write for Your Audience

Using an Easier Reading Selection
- Learn the strategy of **asking questions**

Materials

Student Book

- Reading Workshop, "Asking Questions," pp. 6–15
- Writing Workshop, "Compare-Contrast Essay," pp. 16–21
- Extend, "On Assignment," pp. 22–24

Teacher's Guide Activity Masters

- Reading Selections
  EASY "Celebrating a Good Crop," pp. 29–31
  AVERAGE "Community Life," pp. 32–37
- Graphic Organizer, p. 38
- Comprehension Model, p. 39
- Sample Draft, p. 40

Modeling Transparencies

- Comprehension Transparency A3
- Writing Transparency A4

More Books to Read

Other books that include **compare-contrast writing**:

Reading Expeditions
  China
  Egypt
  Mexico
  Rome

Windows on Literacy
  Harvest Festivals

For more information about the Reading Expeditions and Windows on Literacy series, call 1-800-368-2728.

Before You Begin

Set the Stage

Give groups of students different examples of nonfiction sources about countries of the world. Include encyclopedias, world atlases, books, and children's magazine articles. Have groups skim and scan the sources to notice the types of information contained in each. Then have groups share their observations.

Management Tips

- All students will benefit from teacher modeling of the comprehension strategies.

- Partner less experienced readers with proficient readers during guided practice of the strategies.

- Bring the groups together to share responses.

- See pages 27 and 29–31 for a strategy lesson and a reading selection you can use with less experienced readers.

Introduction

Student Book, page 4

Activate Prior Knowledge

Read aloud the roles of the students on page 4. Ask: *Why is the student confused?* (She doesn't know how to begin writing her essay.)

Discuss what students already know about comparing and contrasting. Write their comments on the board. Ask:

Can you skim through the page again and find a clue word the girl uses to contrast this year and last year? (different)

Student Book, page 5

Teach Comparing and Contrasting

Tell students that when they skimmed the nonfiction materials you gave them, they may have noticed ways the materials were alike and different. Explain that when they notice similarities and differences they are comparing and contrasting.

Draw a Venn diagram on the board. Label each circle with the name of one type of nonfiction materials students previewed; for example, *encyclopedia* and *atlas*. Work with students to complete the diagram.

Explain that students will both read and write an article that compares and contrasts. Read page 5 aloud. Explain that while all nonfiction provides facts, writers can organize their facts in different ways. Comparing and contrasting is one way.

1 Asking Questions

Understand the Strategy

🤓 **Student Book, page 6**

Introduce the Strategy

Ask students to think about why they ask questions. Ask:

When do you ask questions?

Students may mention they ask questions to get help, when they don't understand something, when they need something repeated, and so on.

Read page 6 in the Student Book as a class. Discuss the strategy of asking questions. Clarify that students can ask questions about *how* they read to check up on themselves and about *what* they read to make sure they understand their reading. Make sure students understand the strategies of *rereading* and *reading on*.

📇 **Comprehension Transparency A3***

Model the Strategy

Display Transparency A3 and use it to model the reading strategy.

Today we'll be reading a compare-contrast article about the country of China. As I read, I am going to ask

questions to check how I am doing, to make sure I understand what I read, and to learn more. I will try to answer the questions as I read, but I might not be able to answer them all.

Read the transparency aloud and model asking questions. Stress these steps:

• Ask questions about *how* you read.

• Ask questions about *what* you read.

• Ask questions to learn more.

• Ask questions to find answers, reread, read on, and look for information.

• Remember that some of your questions might not be answered.

---

* Transparencies are available in a separate transparency package and also as Activity Masters at the end of this book. You may wish to create transparencies from these masters.

Comprehension Transparency A3

Asking Questions

❝This subhead tells me that this section is about the Great Wall. What is the Great Wall?❞

THE GREAT WALL

Have you ever heard of the Great Wall of China? It was one of the most famous building projects **in ancient China**. Emperor Shi Huangdi started it. He decided that the wall would protect the northern border of his country.

In 214 B.C., Chinese workers began joining together shorter walls built earlier. Prisoners, slaves, and members of the army helped. It took about ten years to complete the job. That's because the wall was more than 1,500 miles (2,414 kilometers) long!

Later emperors rebuilt the wall using bricks to make it stronger. They also added to the wall until it was about

LOOKING BACK

Many men were needed to build the Great Wall. When someone working on the wall died, the other workers threw the body into the structure and covered it with bricks.

4,500 miles (7,242 kilometers) long. **Today,** people from around the world visit the Great Wall of China.

Now the Chinese are working on another huge building project, the Three Gorges Dam. This **dam** is over 1½ miles (2.4 kilometers) wide. It will control the flow of water, help prevent floods, and create electric power.

❝Do prisoners and the army still build things in China? Maybe I could use the Internet to find the answers.❞

❝Here it says bricks were used to make the wall stronger. What were early walls made out of?❞

❝After reading, I still have questions. *Where is Three Gorges Dam?* I'll have to read on to see if my questions are answered.❞

The Great Wall of China is the longest structure in the world.

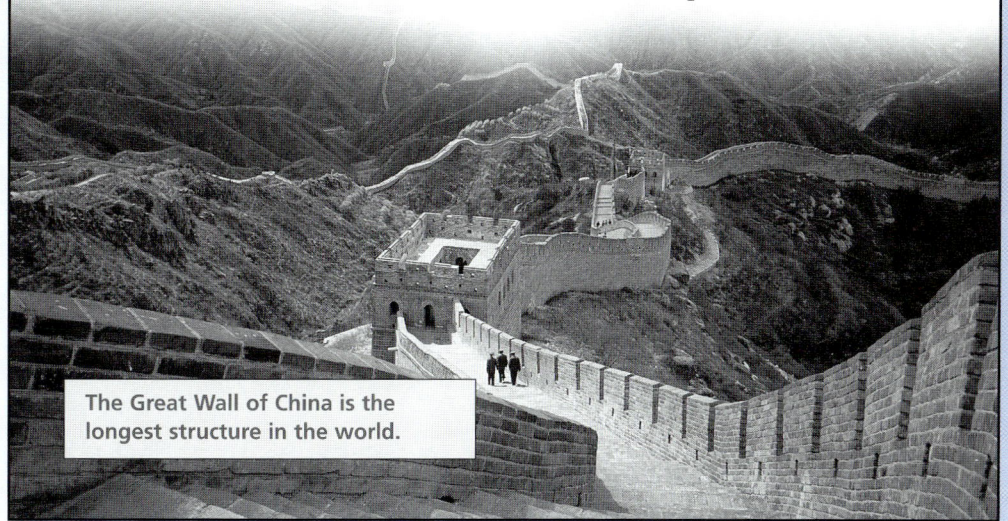

from *China*

Think As You Read

Student Book, page 7

Review the Reading Routine

The five steps on page 7 of the student book provide a routine that good readers use. Students can use this routine before, during, and after they read anything. Review the steps before students read the compare-contrast article on pages 8–13.

Students need to read with a pencil in hand! See "Tools for Taking Notes" for note-taking options. Model for students how to use the tool of your choice.

Practice and Apply the Strategy

Student Book, pages 8–13

ELL Have Students Practice the Strategy

Guided Practice Ask pairs of students to read pages 8–11 and use the questioning strategy. Remind them that asking questions helps them to understand what they read, and so there will be no "right" questions. To guide practice, read the article together, including the margin notes. Explain that these are hints to help them use the strategy. After reading, have volunteers share their notes. Ask:

> Do you have more questions or answers?
> Do you have questions that weren't answered in the article?

Independent Practice Students can read pages 12–13 on their own. These pages do not provide strategy hints, so they can be used as independent practice.

Tools for Taking Notes

Choose one of these note-taking tools for your students to use as they read. Model using the tool for students.

✔ Use sticky notes

Provide students with sticky notes. They can write on them and place them in the margins. Suggest that they code their notes:

Q = My questions
A = Answers

✔ Write in the margins

Provide students with a photocopy of the article on pages 8–13. Students can take their notes by writing in the margins, circling words and phrases, and so on. (See Activity Masters on pages 32–37 of this Teacher's Guide.)

✔ Use a graphic organizer

Provide students with a photocopy of the Activity Master on page 38 of this Teacher's Guide. This is the same graphic organizer shown on page 7 of the student book. Students can write down the questions they have as they read in column 1 and any answers they find in column 2.

Check Understanding

Student Book, page 14

Assess Content

Ask students to read the notes they made as they read "Community Life." Then have them read and complete the Venn diagram on page 14. Model using their notes to synthesize information for the diagram. Some sample responses are shown below.

Review the Strategy

Talk with the class about how they used the questioning strategy. Write down their ideas about how to use the strategy. You might make a chart that shows their ideas and post it so that students can refer to it when they read other compare-contrast articles.

Here's a list of tips one class came up with.

ELL

In Ancient China

- Farmers lived in simple one-story houses, while rich people had bigger houses with two or more floors.
- Only boys went to school, while the girls tended the silkworms.
- Poor people had few foods, while rich people had many different kinds of food.

In Both Ancient and Modern China

- Farmers live in simple houses.
- Farming is important.
- People eat similar foods.

In Modern China

- Both boys and girls go to school.
- China is the largest producer of food in the world.
- People wear modern clothes, like jeans.

ELL

ASKING QUESTIONS

- Ask questions to learn more about the topic.
- Don't worry about asking dumb questions. There are no dumb questions.
- Ask questions about how you're reading to check up on yourself.
- Ask questions about what you're reading so you know you get it.
- Reread, read on, or look for info to answer questions.
- Don't worry if you can't answer all your questions.

Share and Respond

Student Book, page 15

Have Students Share Responses

Ask students to read over the notes they took as they read. Ask:

What information was surprising?
What information was new to you?
What do you still wonder about?

Allow students to work in small groups to share their responses. Remind them that every reader brings his or her own interests and experiences to reading and that talking about our responses to what we read helps everyone learn more about a topic.

Write a Response

Student Book, page 15

Have Students Write a Response

Ask each student to write a response to the article following the instructions on page 15 of the Student Book.

Student responses should include

Information about ancient and modern China from the article, for example,

- similarities in farmers' homes
- differences in school attendance
- continued emphasis on farming

Evidence the student used the strategy, for example,

- the student shares a question he or she still has
- the student mentions rereading, reading on, or looking for information

Evidence of student thinking, for example,

- the student connects information in the article to something he or she already knows
- the student states an opinion about what he or she has read
- the student makes a judgment about what he or she has read
- the student shares any remaining questions

Compare-Contrast Essay

Author's Chair

Student Book, page 16

Share Writing Experiences

To introduce "Author's Chair" on page 16, ask students to think about and share some of their experiences as writers. Ask:

What have you written lately?
How did you decide what to write about?
How did you find information to include?

Read the interview on page 16 with students to discover how the writer of *China*, Kevin Supples, works. As a follow-up, have students interview each other about their writing. First have students work with partners to write a list of questions about writing, for example, *What topics do you know a lot about?* Each pair can then interview another pair of students, using their questions. Tell students the goal is to gather tips for writers.

After students have interviewed each other, collect the tips. Write them on chart paper and post them in the room for students to add to or refer to. Leave space at the bottom so students can add additional tips. Here are some tips one class listed.

ELL

TIPS FOR WRITERS

1. Keep a writer's notebook.
2. Write down ideas, topics, or questions when you think of them.
3. Look at interesting books, videos, and websites to get new information or to find answers to your questions.
4. Get all your ideas down before you try to fix your grammar, spelling, and punctuation.
5. Read aloud your writing to make sure it "sounds" like you.

Prewriting

Student Book, pages 17–18

Discuss Reading/Writing Connection

Have students read the first paragraph and the Reading/Writing Connection on page 17. Explain that the compare-contrast essays they write should include these features. Help students relate each feature to the article they read in Part 1. Ask:

In what ways is the article different from the essay you will write? (Students might answer that the article is part of a book; it uses subheads such as houses, school, and so on). *How is the article similar to the essay you will write?* (Students might answer that they are both compare-contrast essays, or that they both use clue words.)

Model Choosing Subjects to Compare

Generate some pairs of topics you could compare, and list them on the board. Invite students to work as a group to brainstorm a list of pairs of subjects they could compare. Explain that when they brainstorm, students should just list what comes to mind and not worry about what specific details they would write about it. Ask students to look back through their journals to see if there are some interesting subjects they would like to write more about.

Write down some of the ideas. Then go back over the ideas and help students make judgments about how important the topics are to them personally. Remind them that writers choose topics that mean something to them.

Using your own subject or one from the Student Book, model listing details about a pair of subjects. Then ask students to work with partners to list details that compare and contrast their subjects. See *Talking to Young Writers* for more tips.

Talking to Young Writers Tips for helping students choose subjects to compare

Problem	How to Help Students
Student has trouble selecting a pair of subjects to compare and contrast.	Ask the student these questions: • Do you know enough about both subjects? • Can you think of at least 3 ways the subjects are alike and different? • Which subjects do you care the most about? • Which subjects will be interesting to your audience?
Student has trouble selecting whether to compare subjects or compare details.	• Which way best fits how you want to write? • Does one way work better using the details you have written? • How can you use clue words such as *both, neither,* or *only* to compare details or subjects?

Guide Organizing and Planning

Remind students that comparing and contrasting information is one way that writers organize their writing. Students can choose between two methods of organization to find a way of comparing and contrasting that makes sense to them.

Have students turn back to pages 8–13 and look closely at the way the author organized the information in "Community Life." Ask:

Did the author organize the information by subjects or by details? (by details) How would the article look if the author had organized the information by subject? (The author would have put all the information about ancient China together; then he would have put all the information about China today together.)

Read page 18 with students and study together the two ways they can organize their essays. Clarify these points:

- If you organize by subject, you write about all the ways the subjects are alike in one or more paragraphs; then write all the ways the subjects are different.

- If you organize by details, you write how each subject shares or doesn't share the features you have chosen. The features shown on page 18 are foods and fun things to do.

Refer to *Talking to Young Writers* below for tips on clue words and phrases.

Talking to Young Writers **Tips for helping students choose words**

To Signal Similarities	To Signal Differences
• as well as • both • likewise • similarly	• but • instead • however • on the other hand • unlike

Model Writing the First Two Sentences

Model writing the first one or two sentences using your notes or the notes of a student. Talk about whether you are going to organize your essay by subjects or by the details.

Explain that writing the first two sentences of their essays is a way for students to focus their writing. It's a way for them to let their readers know what they will be reading about. Tell students they should introduce the subjects they will compare in the first one or two sentences of their essays.

Drafting

Student Book, page 19

Help Students Start Writing

Model writing an essay of your own using the information you generated earlier. Write quickly, showing students how to get ideas down on paper.

Provide students with time to write. Assure them that there will be time to change and add to their essays, but that getting something down is important.

Revising and Editing

Student Book, pages 20–21

Writing Transparency A4

Activity Master, Teacher's Guide, page 40

Model Revising the Draft

Use the Revising Checklist and Writing Transparency A4 to model making changes to a draft essay. Be sure to point out places that work as well as places where improvements are needed. Sample Think-Alouds for doing this are shown on the facing page. Provide a photocopy of Activity Master on page 40 so students can make their comments and suggestions for change on the draft.

Allow students time to zoom in for a closer look at their essays. (Have they shown in their writing what they want their readers to see?) Have students review their essays and revise and edit them. Copy and distribute the Checklist for a Compare-Contrast Essay (on the inside back cover of this Teacher's Guide) as a final review.

Revising Checklist

- Do I introduce the subjects I will compare?

- Do I explain how each subject is like and different from others?

- Is my essay organized by subjects or by details?

- Do I need more information?

- Have I written a conclusion or did I just stop writing?

Revising and Editing

Favorite Holidays

❝These first two sentences are great. They tell me just what I'm going to read about.❞

Two of my favorite holidays are the Fourth of July and Thanksgiving. Each holiday has great food and fun things to do. Even though Fourth of July and Thanksgiving come at different times of the year, both are school holidays. Also,

all our cousins

~~everybody~~ comes. My dad picks up his mom who lives at a

nursing home. ¶ ~~In the summer us kids sleep outside. On~~
We have great food on both days. We always have turkey.
~~Thanksgiving, we all sleep on the floor.~~ On Turkey day,

Mom and Aunt Liz put the turkey in the oven. ~~Mom cooks the~~

On the Fourth   outside
~~turkey for Thanksgiving in the oven.~~ Dad cooks it on the
                                                ^   ^

grill. ~~One of my aunts is vegetarian so she brings a meatless~~
        ¶ We have lots of fun on each holiday. On the Fourth of July,
~~loaf. Yech! It's gray and funny looking.~~ We all go to the
                                              ^

parade. I used to decorate my bike, but now only Megan,

who is five,
~~whose~~ 5 does it. We always play a big softball game. A

tradition at Thanksgiving is the Toilet Bowl. This is a football

game my uncles and some of their friends ~~from growing up~~

play. ~~Fireworks at the park.~~ Grandma loves Thanksgiving
                                    eat together.   But
because she says it's one meal we all ~~sit down for.~~ I like the
                                        ^   ^
Fourth best because the ~~food is~~ great.
                          ^
              fireworks at the park are

❝This is unclear. It would be good to clarify just who "everybody" is.❞

❝Huh? This is weird. It sounds as if two turkeys are prepared for Thanksgiving. I would change it to make the contrast clear.❞

❝OK. Here the writer is talking about activities, not food. We need a new paragraph. I'm going to write a topic sentence to set up the next part of the essay.❞

Sharing and Publishing

Student Book, page 21

Review with students the Sharing and Publishing options on page 21 of their books. Conference with groups and/or individuals regarding their publishing plans. Students might choose from the following ways to share their writing:

Print Media

- **Make a Book** Students making a group book can look at nonfiction books to get ideas for covers, title page, contents, illustrations, and so on.

Electronic Media

- **School Website** Pairs creating home pages for their essays need to work together to decide on fonts and type sizes that will give their essays contrasting appearances. Help students with other details, such as breaking pages, including folios, scanning in illustrations or photographs, etc.

Performance

- **Author's Chair** Interviews provide students with ways to share not only their writing, but their feelings toward their subjects.

Assess Writing

The following rubric for compare-contrast essays is based on a six-trait model of writing. It represents beginning, developing, and proficient performance.

Scoring Rubric

A well-written article

- Subjects for comparison are clearly stated.
- Organized by subjects or by details.
- Both differences and similarities are identified.
- Directed at fellow students. Voice is natural and conversational.
- Clue words such as *both, each, neither,* and *only* are used.
- Writing is free of mechanical errors.

An average article

- Subjects for comparison are somewhat clearly stated.
- Organization is fairly clear. The chosen approach is not always consistent.
- Both differences and similarities are not always identified.
- Audience is not always clear. Does not have a natural-sounding voice.
- Clue words such as *both, each, neither,* and *only* are not effectively used.
- Writing has some mechanical errors.

A poorly written article

- Subjects for comparison are not stated.
- Organization is not apparent. Details are missing.
- Both differences and similarities are not identified.
- Audience is not clear. Voice is not engaging.
- Clue words such as *both, each, neither,* and *only* are not used.
- Writing has many mechanical errors.

Extend

On Assignment

Student Book, pages 22–24

Review Concepts

Ask students to read "Look Back" on page 22 and think about what they learned in this book. Ask:

What strategy did you learn for reading?
Is anything still confusing?
How might you use this information in reading and writing?

Share responses to the question regarding the students on page 4. (Students might say that learning the characteristics of a compare-contrast article would help the student know how to read and write them.)

Discuss the Assignments

Read over the assignments on pages 22 and 23 with students. Note that the scope of the assignments is smaller than the Writing Workshop, but that each assignment requires students to read and/or write nonfiction text.

Students might work in pairs or small groups to complete the activities. See the chart below for a brief summary of the skills students will use while completing the assignment(s).

Direct students to the list of sources on page 24 of their books. Current Internet sites and books are listed. If possible, spend time perusing these materials with the class.

Use this chart to help make assignments.

ELL Match Assignments and Students	Apply concepts	Research	Synthesize ideas	Use map skills	Use visuals to explain	Express ideas creatively
EASY — **Assignment 1:** Map and label the continents and their locations.	✓	✓	✓	✓	✓	
AVERAGE — **Assignment 2:** Write a compare-contrast essay about a feature of your town in the past and in the present.	✓	✓	✓		✓	✓
CHALLENGING — **Assignment 3:** Create a China Pursuit game.	✓	✓	✓			✓
AVERAGE — **Assignment 4:** Sketch and label a portion of the Great Wall of China.	✓	✓	✓		✓	✓

Meeting Individual Needs

Optional Mini-Lessons

Use the following mini-lessons to help students become more proficient in reading and writing nonfiction.

1 Use Text Features to Predict Content

Lesson Focus Text features help readers access information.

- Ask students to scan pages 8–9. Talk about what they notice first. *What words or phrases pop out? Why?* Point out that the title and subheads are larger than the text and that they are also in darker type. Explain that the title "Community Life" gives the main idea of the article as a whole. The subheads "Houses" and "Schools" show how the article is organized into subtopics.

- Students can use the subheads in the rest of the article to predict content. They can list the subheads for each section to show how the article is organized.

2 ELL Read in Sections

Lesson Focus Reading in smaller pieces helps students keep track of information they read.

- Ask students to look at pages 10–11. Explain that the way the article is laid out on the page makes it easy to read in sections.

- *What clues on the pages help you figure out where good stopping points might be after you read sections? What could you use if there were no subheads?*

- Share strategies you use with students. For example, people often read paragraph-by-paragraph or, page-by-page, or they look for signals, such as fancy characters that signal the beginning and end of text.

3 Write for Your Audience

Lesson Focus Writers need to have an audience in mind before they write.

- Work with students to write a summary of the reading. Tell them the audience is the school principal.

- Then ask the students to rewrite the summary for first or second graders to read.

- Discuss the ways the language in each differs. *What kinds of words would you use for first-graders? For the principal? Why would you change the kinds of words you use?*

- Point out that writers use words that their audiences will understand and find interesting.

Using an Easier Reading Selection

Activity Masters, Teacher's Guide, pages 29–31

Provide students who need an easier reading selection with copies of "Celebrating a Good Crop" on Activity Masters 29–31.

Activate Prior Knowledge

Preview the article with students, pointing out the title, subheads, and illustrations. Ask:

What questions do you have about the article? Let's write them down and see if they are answered as we read.

Model the Strategy

Model for students how to use the **questioning** strategy. Think aloud as you read "Celebrating a Good Crop." Use the margin notes on the first page as a guide. (See strategy steps on page 14 of this Teacher's Guide.)

Guide Practice

Guide students as they read and take notes. You may want to read the entire article aloud first with students modeling your questions.

Then have students use the strategy as they read the article. Encourage students to read the article in sections and take time to review their questions and answers as they finish each section. Stress that students might not find the answers to all their questions in their reading.

Assess

Ask students to share their notes. You might draw a chart like the one shown here on the board. Invite students to explain how they found the answers to their own questions.

Then ask students to look back over the article and locate all the subheads. Explain that the subheads can be used to group facts students learned from the article. Write the heads "Celebrating Holi" and "The Yam Festival" on the board. Work with students to identify which facts from the chart can be sorted into which category.

My Questions	Answers

Activity Masters

Contents

Activity Master	Purpose
Activity Masters 29–31 Reading Selection *EASY* "Celebrating a Good Crop" from *Harvest Festivals*	• Provides more practice in using the strategy. • Provides strategy instruction for less experienced readers.
Activity Masters 32–37 Reading Selection *AVERAGE* "Community Life" from *China*	• Provides a copy of the article in the Student's Book. With this copy, students can take notes right on the text.
Activity Master 38 Graphic Organizer	• Provides a note-taking tool students can use during reading.
Activity Master 39 Comprehension Model	• Provides a copy of the Transparency used to model the Comprehension Strategy. You can use this to make your own transparency or you can provide a copy to students to follow along as you model the strategy.
Activity Master 40 Sample Draft	• Provides a copy of the Transparency used to model Revising and Editing. You can use this to make your own transparency or you can provide a copy to students to follow along as you model the strategy.

Reading Strategy: Asking Questions

As you read, ask questions to make sure you're getting what the article is about. Ask other questions to learn more about the subjects. Write your questions along the sides of the article. Look for information that answers them. Not all your questions will be answered. Use the notes to help you.

> The title tells what this section is about.

Celebrating a Good Crop

People all over the world celebrate after crops are harvested. Farming is hard work. First, farmers plow their fields. Then, they plant the seeds and wait for them to grow. After months of hard work, it is time to harvest the crops. Then it is time to celebrate. Most harvest festivals include singing, dancing, giving thanks, and, of course, lots of good food.

> When are the celebrations? Are they in our country too?

> What does *Holi* mean?

Celebrating Holi

People in India celebrate the festival of Holi in March. This festival takes place after the wheat harvest. Wheat is an important crop. It is used to make flour, bread, cereal, and other foods.

Directions

Read this page to learn more about Holi. Keep writing down
questions you have. Look for the answers too.

> People light bonfires the night before Holi begins.
> According to legend, long ago a king wanted to
> be worshipped like a god. But the king's son,
> Prahlad, chose to worship the god Vishnu. This
> made the king very angry. He ordered Prahlad to
> be killed. Prahlad's evil sister, Holika, led Prahlad
> into a bonfire. Everyone thought Prahlad would
> die. Vishnu saved Prahlad. Holika died instead.
> The festival of Holi is named after Holika.
>
> Holi is a favorite festival of the children. During
> the festival, everyone dusts themselves with
> brightly colored powders. The colored powders are
> called *gulal*. Then, people squirt each other with
> water. Soon, everyone is covered with bright colors.

| This explains what *Holi* means. |

| Does the color ever wear off? |

Name ....

Directions
Read to the end of the article. What new questions do you have?
Are you finding answers to some of your questions?

The Yam Festival

Ghana is a country in Africa. People here celebrate the yam festival in the fall. This festival celebrates the yam harvest. Yams are an important crop in Ghana.

The yam festival lasts a week. It is a time when farmers honor the gods that watched over their crops.

In the forest, the first yams are taken from the ground. The farmers carry the yams to the village. The yams are then blessed and given to the chief. The chief has them cooked and shares them with everyone in the village. ❖

Think About What You Read
Do you still have questions about what you read? Write down what you still wonder about how people celebrate when their crops are harvested.

I wonder _____

_____

_____

Name ....

Practice and Apply the Strategy

Ask questions as you read about community life in China. Then read on to see if your questions are answered. The margin notes include questions one reader asked.

> The title tells me the topic of the article.

> The subhead tells me what this section is about.

> The words "In ancient China" and "Today" are clue words. They point to a comparison or contrast coming up.

> Q: Wooden pillows! How could they ever get to sleep?

COMMUNITY LIFE 福風亭

►HOUSES

In ancient China, three generations of a family often lived together in one house. There were rules about how family members acted. Children were taught to obey their parents. The grandparents, as the oldest, were the most respected.

Most people in ancient China were farmers. Farmers lived in simple one-story houses. The roofs were made of straw. Families slept on simple mats. They used wooden pillows. Houses had outdoor areas for cooking.

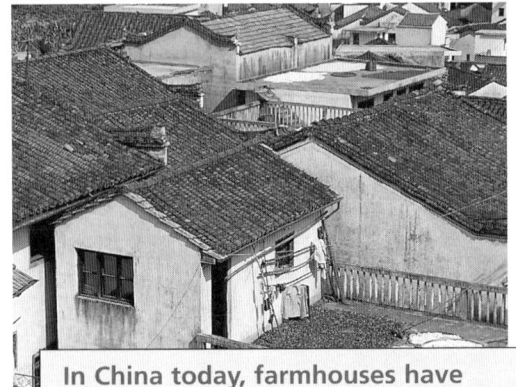

In China today, farmhouses have tile or straw roofs and are built of stone or clay bricks.

We know a lot more about the homes of the rich. The rich were sometimes buried with a clay model of their home. Their houses had two or more floors and tile roofs.

LOOKING BACK

Did you know that the ancient Chinese did not use stone to build their houses? They used wood or bamboo, a tall, woody plant that grows in many places in China. The Chinese sometimes covered the walls with bricks or earth.

Today, Chinese farmers live in simple houses like those of long ago. Their houses are small and have few pieces of furniture. Toilets are outside. In the cities, most people live in crowded apartments. The apartments are built around courtyards. People living in an apartment building share the courtyard. Some apartments do not have baths. So, people use public baths in the cities.

This section will be about school.

Here are the clue words "In ancient China" and "Today" again. So what is coming up? It must be either a comparison or a contrast.

SCHOOL

Do you think you would like being a scholar? You would spend all your time studying and learning. Scholars were the most respected group in ancient times. Scholars could read and write. Most worked for the emperor, the ruler of the country.

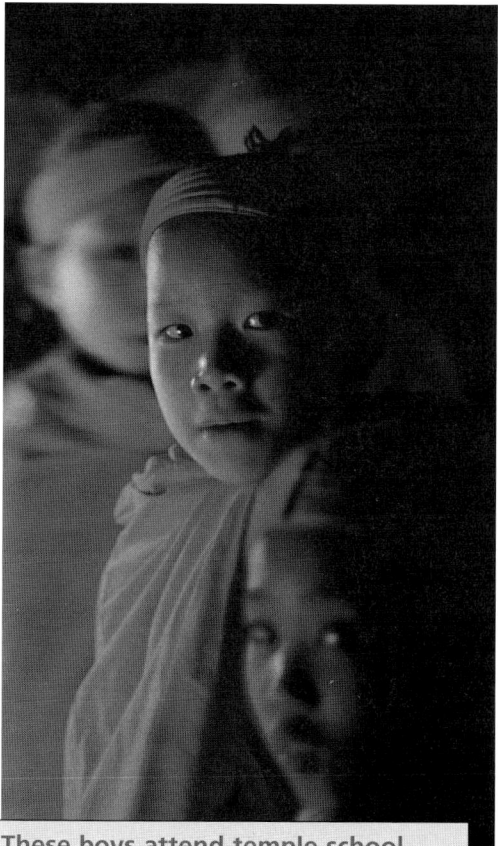

LOOKING BACK

Working for the government was a good job. But very few could get this job. In later years, the odds of passing the palace test and getting a job were 3,000 to one!

In ancient China, only boys were educated. Sometimes a whole village would choose one young boy to become a scholar. This boy would then go on to the university. He would work for the emperor or in the government, called the Imperial Civil Service.

Q: In ancient China, girls didn't go to school. I wonder: Do girls go to school in China today?

Girls learned to take care of the house. They also learned about silk. They learned how to raise silkworms which spun silk thread. The silk industry in China was developed and run by women.

Today, almost all children in China go to school. They start school at age six or seven. Children in the cities go to school for six full days each week. They have six weeks of vacation during the summer. They also have four weeks off in the winter. Children in the country take time off from school to work on the farms.

A: Girls do go to school today. It says right here that almost all children go to school, so that includes girls.

These boys attend temple school.

Practice and Apply
the Strategy

What questions do you have as you read these two pages? Remember to write them down. Write down the answers you find too. One reader's questions are shown here.

This section is about farming.

Here are "In ancient China" and "Today" again. They point to a comparison or contrast coming up.

Q: What does a rice paddy look like?

A: So this is what a rice paddy looks like. But are the rice plants growing under all the water? Does the water just soak into the ground?

► **FARMING**

In ancient China, many people lived in the country. They were farmers. They lived in small villages. Farmers were well respected in China. Farmers worked from dawn to dusk.

In northern China, farmers grew beans and grain, including wheat and barley. In the south, farmers grew rice in special fields called paddies. They flooded these fields with water from nearby rivers.

In early China, farmers used oxen to pull plows. They also used iron tools. They invented the wheelbarrow, which they called a "wooden ox." These improvements helped people farm better.

LOOKING BACK

Everyone in ancient China had to pay taxes. Farmers often paid their taxes with rice. They could also pay by working for the government, digging canals, or building walls. Farmers had to join the army for a period of time.

Today, farming is still important in China. More than half of the people in China are farmers or work on farms. China is the largest producer of food in the world. It has to feed over one billion people. Grain, such as rice and wheat, is China's most important crop. Large farms are run by the government. Much of the land is also owned by the government.

A water buffalo and farmers leave rice paddy fields in the evening.

Q: Will I be reading about the kind of Chinese food that we get in restaurants?

FOOD

In ancient China, poor families ate beans, other vegetables, and grains. They did not usually eat meat. Sometimes they ate chicken, fish, or wild birds. To save fuel, they chopped their food into small pieces. Then they cooked the pieces quickly in an iron frying pan, or wok. Families also steamed their food.

Rich families ate many different foods. Noodles, fruits, and vegetables were popular. Honey, cinnamon, peanuts, ginger, and salt added flavor to food. The rich also ate meat, including pork, deer, duck, and lamb. They even enjoyed eating snake, dog, and bear paws!

Tea was the most important drink. Some people became experts on tea. There were tea-tasting contests. Experts tried to tell which tea they were tasting.

Today, many Chinese eat some of the same foods that families ate long ago. Breakfast is often noodles, wheat bread, or rice porridge. The porridge is topped with shrimp, vegetables, or pickles.

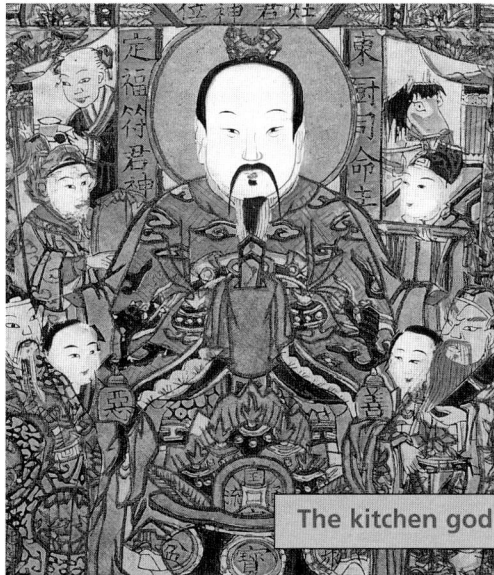

The kitchen god

LOOKING BACK

The kitchen god was important in ancient China. The Chinese believed that the kitchen god reported how a family behaved during the year to the other gods. A bad report could mean bad luck for the next year. Families set off fireworks to honor the kitchen god.

The Chinese eat with chopsticks and soup spoons. They use knives only in the kitchen, not at the table. Silverware is thought to be in bad taste. Meals are either stir-fried in woks or steamed.

Q: Where do chopsticks come from?

A: We eat stir-fry, but not porridge. That sounds like something they eat in fairy tales.

Practice and Apply the Strategy

Continue reading and asking questions. Be sure you write down your questions and any answers you find. Remember that some questions may not be answered. You may need to do further research to answer them.

CLOTHES

In ancient China, you could tell who was rich and who was poor by the clothes they wore. The poor wore clothes made from hemp. Hemp is a rough fabric woven from plant fibers. Clothes were loose with tunic-like tops and simple pants.

The rich wore robes made from silk. They also wore jewelry made of jade, gold, and silver. Sometimes men wore hats. A hat showed the wearer's job and social class.

Wealthy men in China used to wear fancy silk robes and hats.

LOOKING BACK

The colors of cloth were important to the ancient Chinese. Cloth was colored with vegetable dyes. Each color meant something special. Yellow was a royal color. Only the emperor could wear it. Other people dressed in blue or black. White was for mourning. Children could not wear white while their parents were still alive. Red was the color of luck.

The ancient Chinese thought that women should have very small feet. It was a sign of beauty. Girls had their feet bound so that their feet would not grow. This painful practice was stopped in 1902.

Today, many Chinese wear Western-style shirts and loosely fitting pants or dark suits that button at the neck. In the country, farmers wear clothes that are like those peasants wore long ago.

In cities, people tend to wear more modern clothes. Jeans, however, are very expensive. Some people have to save for a year to buy a pair of jeans. Few people wear silk.

Chinese men carry a paper dragon in a New Year's parade.

FESTIVALS AND GAMES

In ancient China, festivals and games were important. The most important festival was held at the New Year. This holiday lasted 15 days. Families got together. Relatives came from far away. People visited each other bringing gifts. It was considered bad luck to turn away visitors. The holiday ended with a parade that included dragons and lanterns. The Chinese believed that the dragon would bring good luck for the New Year.

Another important festival was Qingming. During this festival people honored their dead relatives. People brought food to the graves and "talked" to their relatives. They wished them good lives in the afterworld.

Children had little time for games. Most children worked on the farms. But during festivals they flew kites and played chess and Chinese checkers. They also had a toy that is like our modern yo-yo.

Today, the Chinese New Year is still a popular holiday. Chinese around the world celebrate it. Chinese New Year starts no earlier than January 20 and no later than February 20. There are fireworks and parades with huge paper dragons. Children receive red envelopes with money and sometimes oranges for good luck.

Taking Notes

Directions
Use this chart as you read. Write your questions in the first column and the answers in the second column. You may not find all the answers to your questions. As you read, think how you might find some of the answers.

My Questions	Answers

Name .... **Compare-Contrast Article**

Comprehension Model

THE GREAT WALL

Have you ever heard of the Great Wall of China? It was one of the most famous building projects **in ancient China**. Emperor Shi Huangdi started it. He decided that the wall would protect the northern border of his country.

In 214 B.C., Chinese workers began joining together shorter walls built earlier. Prisoners, slaves, and members of the army helped. It took about ten years to complete the job. That's because the wall was more than 1,500 miles (2,414 kilometers) long!

Later emperors rebuilt the wall using bricks to make it stronger. They also added to the wall until it was about

LOOKING BACK

Many men were needed to build the Great Wall. When someone working on the wall died, the other workers threw the body into the structure and covered it with bricks.

4,500 miles (7,242 kilometers) long. **Today**, people from around the world visit the Great Wall of China.

Now the Chinese are working on another huge building project, the Three Gorges Dam. This dam is over 1½ miles (2.4 kilometers) wide. It will control the flow of water, help prevent floods, and create electric power.

The Great Wall of China is the longest structure in the world.

Name .... **Compare-Contrast Article**

Sample Draft

Revising a Draft

Directions

Read this draft of a compare-contrast essay about favorite holidays.
Use the Revising Checklist on page 20 of the Student Book and
make changes. Share your revising ideas with a partner.

Favorite Holidays

Two of my favorite holidays are the Fourth of July and
Thanksgiving. Each holiday has great food and fun things to
do. Even though Fourth of July and Thanksgiving come at
different times of the year, both are school holidays. Also,
everybody comes. My dad picks up his mom who lives at a
nursing home. In the summer us kids sleep outside. On
Thanksgiving, we all sleep on the floor. On Turkey day,
Mom and Aunt Liz put the turkey in the oven. Mom cooks the
turkey for Thanksgiving in the oven. Dad cooks it on the
grill. One of my aunts is vegetarian so she brings a meatless
loaf. Yech! It's gray and funny looking. We all go to the
parade. I used to decorate my bike, but now only Megan,
whose 5 does it. We always play a big softball game. A
tradition at Thanksgiving is the Toilet Bowl. This is a football
game my uncles and some of their friends from growing up
play. Fireworks at the park. Grandma loves Thanksgiving
because she says it's one meal we all sit down for. I like the
Fourth best because the food is great.